Who Will Love Me?

Who Will Love Me?

A Holistic Approach to Building
Meaningful Relationships
After Sexual Assault

Melissa Ann McDaniel

NEW YORK

LONDON • NASHVILLE • MELBOURNE • VANCOUVER

Who Will Love Me?

A Holistic Approach to Building Meaningful Relationships
After Sexual Assault

Published in New York, New York, by Morgan James Publishing. Morgan James is a trademark of Morgan James, LLC. www.MorganJamesPublishing.com

The author has tried to recreate events, locales, and conversations from her memories of them. In order to maintain their anonymity in some instances, she has changed the names of individuals and places. She may have changed some identifying characteristics and details such as physical properties, occupations and places of residence.

ISBN 978-1-64279-759-6 paperback
ISBN 978-1-64279-760-2 eBook
Library of Congress Control Number: 2019912148

Cover Design by:
Rachel Lopez
www.r2cdesign.com

Interior Design by:
Bonnie Bushman
The Whole Caboodle Graphic Design

Editing:
Bethany Davis

Proofreading:
Janina Lawrence

Author's photo courtesy of:
Emily Wenzel Photography

Morgan James is a proud partner of Habitat for Humanity Peninsula
and Greater Williamsburg. Partners in building since 2006.

Get involved today! Visit
www.MorganJamesBuilds.com

Dedication

For my little (big) sister, Chelsey.

At nineteen years of age, you bravely held my hand while I tearfully read my impact statement to a full courtroom. Our relationship is beyond the definition of meaningful, and I am forever grateful to have you by my side.

Love you mucho,
Your big (little) sister,
Melissa Ann

Table of Contents

Acknowledgements

This book would not be possible without the brave and powerful people who have come before me. I cannot fully express my admiration for those who have led the way in creating movements to support others to speak up and step out into the light after sexual assault. You inspire me daily.

To the wonderful faculty and staff in Salve Regina University's master of arts in holistic leadership program, thank you. Your wisdom and grace held the space for me to grow into the woman and leader I am today.

Dr. Angela Lauria and the AI team, you made this woman's dreams come true. Thank you for loving me unconditionally as I laughed, cried, and wrote my way to becoming the author and difference maker I was destined to be.

To my country bumpkin family, from the times we dressed our pigs up at the county fair to the occasions we baked pies at Grandma School, you have taught me the importance of determination and perseverance. My work ethic and desire to pave new ways stem from you.

Introduction

Dear reader,

This is my love letter to you.

Do you often feel anomalous? Do you find yourself wondering, "Who will love me?" Many times after being sexually assaulted, you can feel immense loneliness and isolation. You may find yourself wearing the face of perfection at work, only to come home and fall to pieces. There may be times you long for the ability to trust a new love interest, but find yourself unsure of how to let somebody in again. Your family might occasionally say, "Why are you SO sensitive?" making you feel misunderstood and as if you don't belong.

If any of these statements sound like you, please know that you are not alone.

So, who am I and what do I know about the affects sexual assault can have on building meaningful relationships?

Well, simply put, I am you. The woman who consistently questioned, "Who will love me?" after being sexually assaulted; the woman who has fallen to the floor while doing the dishes because the painful weight after is too much to bear; the woman who has tried to hide her feelings from others and herself, which eventually has forced me to lead two separate lives.

I often told the story of the overly educated, well-traveled millennial with the world at her fingertips because it made me feel significant. The real life I lived included all the above, but also consisted of deep feelings of shame, self-hate, and disgust. I found phenomenal ways to divert conversations and build phony relationships because I was terrified about what friends, partners, and family would think if they truly knew who I was inside. I hated my body. If there was a way to purchase a new one, I would have been the first in line!

Sick and tired, literally and figuratively, I made it my personal mission to explore different healing modalities from around the world. Meeting with a Tanzanian spiritual healer was my first glimpse into new ways of thinking. Our meeting propelled me forward into believing healing and meaningful relationships are possible. After Tanzania, my next adventure landed me on the little island of Skopelos, Greece, where I learned self-love might not be bad. These cultural perspectives began to create a paradigm shift in my thinking and my life. I was not able to fully articulate how those adventures shaped me until I was called to attend the Holistic Leadership graduate program at Salve Regina University. It was there my newfound perspectives began to come to life.

Now I find myself with a beautiful box of tools equipped with lovely affirmations, ways to catch myself before I fall to the kitchen floor, and a fierce love for my rockin' body. All of these tools have supported me to build the meaningful relationships I so missed and desired after being sexually assaulted. They have helped myself and many others learn the answer to the question, "Who will love me?"

This book has been written with my whole heart. It is intended to give you the space and love you need to move beyond loneliness and isolation and into a world of truly meaningful relationships.

I see you. I hear you. I love you. I am you.

With my whole heart,
Love,
Melissa Ann

Chapter 1
Not Ready to Make Nice

Is It Love?

The rarely seen May sunshine sparkled on the beautiful bay outside my picture window. Hit with a terrible spring cold, I was confined to my secondhand futon with an oversized box of tissues marveling out at the beauty. Lonely and wanting company, I invited the handsome six feet three man I had recently started seeing to come over and hang out.

He replied, "Going to the gym and then I'm on my way."

Excitement swirled as I awaited his arrival. There is no better feeling than the butterflies of a new love interest. The handsome man arrived at my apartment with beautiful blue flowers from his garden, a guitar to accompany his love songs, and chicken noodle soup to heal my awful cold. What a dream!

We spent the evening talking about life and our goals for the future. I was twenty and had the whole world ahead of me. I dreamt of traveling to countries only seen in *National Geographic*, while he aspired to be a famous chef. Although we only spent time together a handful of times, the conversations never seemed forced or awkward. Our words flowed naturally.

When the gourmet chicken noodle soup "out of the can" was ready, he invited me to come to the table. I sat there grateful for my chicken noodle soup and for the man who had prepared it. Halfway into dinner, overwhelming exhaustion took over my body. My head became too heavy for my neck to bear its weight. I gently laid my head in my hands. Confused and out of sorts, I chose to go to bed, leaving the handsome man in my living room to fend for himself.

I awoke in the early morning hours to find him still awake in my living room. Strange! It was too early to send him home, so I invited him "just" to go to bed. Shortly after he came to bed, he raped me. I will not share all the graphic details except this: as I tried to push the six feet three muscular man off of my five feet six small frame, he explained why he was raping me, "because I love you." WTF!

Slow Motion and Little Commotion

The minutes after he raped me felt like a video playing in slow motion. Most might assume my apartment was filled with screams of terror and anger; instead, I quietly rose from bed and slowly made my way to the bathroom. The look on his face was of sheer satisfaction as he watched me wipe the tears from my cheeks. He just conquered the world while destroying mine. Not wanting to go back to the bed where the rapist sat, I meekly walked into the living room for some space to breathe. Trying to provide comfort and letting me know the rape was a form of love, the man followed right behind, leaving me no space for me to catch my breath or process what had happened.

My next reaction is still a mystery. There was no energy left in my body to retaliate. I chose to leave the rapist in my living room and return to bed, shutting the door behind me for protection. How did such a strong, vocal young woman react so nonchalantly? Your guess is as good as mine; there is plenty of room for interpretation about what may have been in my chicken noodle soup.

The Morning After

When I woke up the next morning, the man was nowhere to be found. All that remained in my apartment were the wilted blue flowers, his guitar, and so much guilt. Immediately, I began to blame myself, only for 50 percent though. That seemed fair. My invitation for him to go to bed must have been too much for his male hormones to handle. My "no" and "stop" must have been too meek and appeared flirtatious. After all, I kissed him. Keeping my underwear on was no indication of not wanting him inside me. Clearly the appropriate thing for him to do in that situation was to pull my pink panties over and roughly shove it in.

Out of sorts and feeling half dead, I sent the man an email. We knew each other well enough to exchange emails. Let that sink in. In my email, I said it was partially my fault because I let him into my bed. If I owned my part, it made it feel slightly less like the actual rape it was.

To Report or Not to Report?

The first person I told was my dear friend Aundra. She bravely held the space for me to talk about the parts I could and reassured me, "No, this is not your fault." Wanting the man's stuff out of my apartment, Aundra and I got in her blue Suzuki and delivered his guitar. In blaming myself, I also felt the need to "do the right thing" by returning his belongings.

In my heart, however, I knew the next step was to report the rape to the police, but I died a little inside each time I went to reach for the phone. For me, reporting the rape meant I had to own it actually happened. Things like this do not happen to women like me. Right?!

At the time, I was attending university on a full-ride scholarship. Seeking help, I went to the first school counselor with an opening. Meekly walking into the office, I was greeted by a timid woman with brown hair. To the best of my ability, I told her my story with tears in my eyes and a tissue in hand.

The advice the counselor gave to me went something like this: "Melissa, if you choose to report the rape, police typically don't do anything. The experience is often worse for the victim if she does report. But, ultimately it is your choice."

All I wanted was for someone to tell me what to do: *How do I handle this situation?* Instead, the decision to report or not was left up to me. It was a decision that I did not feel I had the capacity to make.

The timid brown-haired woman wrote a note for my math professor to excuse me from the missed classes and sent me on my way. The note included nothing about the sexual assault, just that I should be excused from the absences.

Walking down the hall to meet with my math professor, all I could think about was my lack of ability to advocate for myself. How do I tell my male math professor something like this? It was also one more indicator to confirm in my heart that in fact, I had been raped.

The math professor was a tall, slender, white male who wore little expression on his face. After reading the note, he looked at me and said, "Anyone can get a note from the school counselor for anything. You are not excused."

At these words, I started sobbing and asked him if I could share what happened. Nope! He told me he didn't care and the absences were not excused. When I left his office, what had been left of my heart was shattered in a million pieces.

Not sure where to turn, I called the timid brown-haired counselor and notified her of the interaction. Never again would I return to the math class. An "F" sounded better to me than ever seeing him again. I'm not sure how it was communicated via the school, but the professor must have received the message loud and clear to excuse me. I never went back to the class and still received a "C-" on my transcript.

Report!

According to the National Sexual Violence Resource Center (NSVRC), "Rape is the most under reported crime; 63 percent of sexual assaults are not reported to police."

And then the day came when I had to make the dreaded call. It was a handful of days after the rape, and one of my girlfriends saw the rapist creepily riding his bicycle on the university campus. He was peering through his sunglasses, looking around, and trying to locate me. Yes, he also had already met my friends prior to raping me. At the moment my friend notified me, I knew I had to call the police.

My dear friend Kathleen, and her gentle spirit sat beside me as I called 911. When the officer arrived, I felt conflicting senses of relief and terror. I was still not sure how to own this being my real life?! Unlike my interaction with the math professor, the male police officer was kind throughout his questioning, and made me feel safe. He took my statement and went on his way.

Kathleen then gave me a big hug and also went on her way. Home alone with my despair, I attempted to get some sleep.

I've Reported; Now What?

A whirlwind happened after I reported the crime. I went home to tell my family I had been raped, but I did not say a word despite my intent. I literally spent a whole three days in their company with my lips sealed. Telling them would be another acknowledgement I actually had been raped. My heart could not handle anymore.

After my secret-filled family weekend, I made the five-hour drive back to the city on the bay, berating myself the whole way. My head kept filling with the accusations that I assumed my family would make if I told them. *Surely they, too, will say it is my fault? What was I thinking in asking a man to go to sleep in my bed, assuming he would not have his way with me?*

Upon my arrival, I was greeted by phone calls from detectives asking me to come to the station and identify mug shots. *Holy crap!* … His photo was in the group of mug shots.

It was a younger version, but most definitely him. Next, the detectives asked me to show them where the man lived.

It felt like a scene from the movies. Lying down in the back of the undercover detective car was an adventure in itself. I remember feeling foolish as I asked, "Do I need to wear my seatbelt correctly? I can't wear it and lay down in the back of the car." *Ha!* Clearly the detectives did not care. They were more concerned with keeping me hidden and safe as I directed them to the rapist's house.

Quickly, I learned this man was any female's nightmare. Prior to raping me, he had already raped a minor in a different state and was on parole for the conviction. *HE WAS NOT SUPPOSED TO BE IN WASHINGTON STATE.* Everything he told me had been a lie, from his age to his profession. There was no ounce of truth to anything he had said. The only truthful thing he told me was his full name.

Victim Blaming Is Real

After learning this information, I knew I had to tell my family. It was one of the most difficult phone calls I have had to make in my life. The family members I spoke to encouraged me to make the five-hour drive home to decide what to do next.

Sitting in the small living room, a family meeting was called to order. I was asked to disclose what had happened. Terrified, convinced they were going to blame me, I shared as much of the rape as I could.

Sadly, there were comments of blame, words like, "Why would you let him in your apartment?" and "You asked him to go to bed? That's just asking for it."

My flight response was in high gear at these words, and I was ready to flee. The self-blame took on an all-time high after this conversation. My family had to be right. *Maybe I had been asking for it?*

Cutting my family out at this point would have been ideal, but I still needed the small amount of support they were able to offer. Some support was better than nothing at this point. One of my go-to sayings when trying to understand others is, "Hurt people, hurt people." Being further removed from the situation, I am now able to see the effects of historical abuse and the ramifications it can have through generations if not addressed and healed. They hurt me because they too were hurting.

Rapist, Where Are You?

Due to the police's inability to locate the man, my family encouraged me to move to a new city for my own safety.

The Dixie Chicks' song "Not Ready to Make Nice" gave me strength to pack up my belongings as I lethargically moved around my apartment. My organizational skills were not on point. I'm pretty sure I packed the refrigerated food with my shoes. Leaving a city I so greatly loved felt like another piece of me the rapist was stealing, and I did not know how to handle it.

My grandmother was on her way to help, which felt like a huge relief. A knock on the door meant someone would be there to help unravel this mess.

When the knock came, I was surprised to find my father at the door. At this time, I had no idea he even knew I had been raped. I was grateful to see him. He seemed more shook up than me. Together our packing skills were hilarious. Grandma arrived and we loaded the pickup truck up like a game of Tetris.

Restraining Order

The county chose not to pursue my case because they felt there was not enough evidence. I reported the event days after the rape; I did not have the dreaded rape kit done, and I sent the rapist an email saying I was 50 percent to blame. To say I carried the guilt of this event around for years is an understatement. *Why wasn't I strong enough to report? Why did I blame myself enough to write an email?*

Although the police were not going to pursue my case, they still encouraged me to get a restraining order. Every two weeks, I drove back to the city on the bay to renew my temporary restraining order. The five-hour drive felt like a death sentence. *Why haven't they found him? Will they ever find him?*

Every night I cried and prayed to any god or goddess that would listen, *please find him*. And then one day the call finally came, but the tone in the detective's voice was less than cheery.

He told me, "Melissa, I have good news and I have bad news. The good news is we have located the rapist. The bad news is we found him because he did it to somebody else."

My heart sank.

I'll never forget that day. I was in my mom's driveway, and all I could do was walk over to the trampoline and lay down. Tears streamed down my face while I looked blankly up at the blue sky.

A myriad of thoughts consumed my mind. *It was my fault she had been raped. If I had reported my rape sooner, then he would have been in jail, and she would have never had to go through this, too. I'm such a fucking wimp. Why didn't I speak up sooner? Because I couldn't handle speaking up, someone else had to be raped.* The dark thoughts went on and on.

I listened to "Not Ready to Make Nice" on repeat as I made the five-hour drive to my final restraining order hearing. It was my power jam.

The most wonderful legal advocate supported me in the courtroom so that I did not have to be there alone. Some family members chose not to go with me; others I chose not to invite because I could not sit in the courtroom next to their victim-shaming words.

When the rapist walked into the room, he was wearing a jumpsuit, handcuffs, and the face of a monster. He continuously stared at me, periodically shaking his head like he wanted to jump from the witness stand and rape me again. The rapist behaved so badly that the deputies were also scared for me. They each reassured me that when the court planned to adjourn again in two weeks, there would be extra protection for me.

That's right. We had to meet again. The rapist wanted legal representation to proceed with the restraining order. *Ugh!* As officials took him out of the courtroom, my skin crawled. I drove the five hours back to my hometown with a measly short-term restraining order.

The final time (or so I thought) the same legal advocate sat in the courtroom pews with me. She was pure love and strength. Additionally, the court placed a deputy at either side of the pew I was in, one at the door, and two to be near him. Although it felt great to feel surrounded by their strength, his piercing eyes still cut right into me.

I was granted a restraining order that would last until the other victim's trial was complete. This concession felt a million times better than the biweekly driving I had been doing. I left thinking my legal obligation was done. I also wondered how the other victim was doing and what would become of her trial. At this time, we were not able to speak.

Determination and Depositions

Determined not to lose my full-ride scholarship and to be a first-generation college graduate, I chose to relocate to a new city filled with other colleges and universities. I immediately enrolled in the community college to complete my associate transfer degree.

While going to the community college, I received a phone call from an attorney asking to speak with me. *What? I thought everything was over.* However, they wanted me to testify in the other woman's trial as a character witness. Still feeling the guilt and shame for allowing the rapist to rape another woman, I said yes with no hesitation. I had to support her and get this man locked up.

The commitment, however, opened up a whole new level of *Oh s****. Weekly and sometimes daily, I received phone calls from the attorneys. Trying to differentiate between whom I could talk to and whom I could not was draining. During this time, I had the support of the most wonderful mental health counselor. In her office, I cried my tears and tried to make sense of the pain.

Originally a person I respected greatly advised me not to tell anyone, except the police and my counselor. *People would judge me, think less of me, and talk about me behind my back. I would no longer be perceived as perfect. Heaven forbid.*

As a result, I handled most legal issues, life, school, and relationships with the idea that my true feelings had to be kept secret. Nobody could know I was in pain or talking to attorneys. To the outside world, I was simply a college student, working at the Bee's, and living her best life.

Eventually, the phone calls from attorneys and the isolation were all more than my body, mind, and spirit could handle. I called the prosecuting attorney and said I was done. There was no way I could continue down this path. Feeling like I let the other woman down once again, I just didn't know how to go on alone.

Subpoenaed

And then I was subpoenaed. My cry to refuse going any further with the process, which really equated to a cry for help and wanting out, did not matter. Shortly after, attorneys were flying to the city where I then lived to take my deposition.

The day before the deposition, I met with the prosecuting attorney, a victim advocate, and my counselor. During the meeting, I shared with them my story, and they briefed me on what a deposition is. Ready or not, tomorrow was coming, and I just had to hope for the best. My mind, spirit, and body were not sure they could handle anymore, but they did not have a choice.

As I entered the small room in the courthouse, I felt my body begin to tremble. My mind was fighting with itself with a series of opposing thoughts: *You can't do this. Pull it together... you have to do this. You are such a wimp. Find your inner strength.*

Six of us packed into the small room: the prosecuting attorney, defense attorney, victim advocate, myself, my counselor, and the stenographer. All I remember is the defense attorney tearing me down to make me feel like the smallest human on the planet. I was never able to complete my sentences, let alone a thought.

Sobbing, I ran (more like sprinted) out of the small room and into the bathroom. I then fell on the disgusting bathroom floor, trembling and crying so hard that I was unable to breathe. Nobody warned me I would need my inhaler for a deposition!

People in the courthouse popped their heads out of their office to make sure I was okay. It was so embarrassing. I left feeling as if I was the most insignificant person in the world. Both my counselor and the prosecuting attorney apologized to me for not making the deposition stop. They said it was the worst attack of a victim they had ever seen.

Pedicures and nachos were on the agenda for the evening with my mom, some of my favorite things. I cried through the whole pedicure. Even the smallest touch of my toe felt like an intrusion into my body. Nachos had also been one of my favorite foods; that night, I ate two bites and cried again. Food was also not on the list of things I liked after the deposition. All I wanted to do was go home, curl up, and cry. Although my mom asked what had happened at the deposition, I had no energy or will to explain it to her. I was done…with everything.

Not feeling able to talk to anyone in my life about what was really going on made maintaining or building meaningful relationships a train wreck. The people I opened up to were few and far between. Constantly, I wondered, if people saw through my comedic conversations and the many masks I wore to hide the pain. A conversation deeper than the weather or how work was going felt like an interrogation into the secret life of Melissa. My life lost its authenticity, and I lost my ability to feel human. I specifically remember a conversation with my cousin; she called to see if I wanted to hang out. I flat out lied, saying I had to study. Little did she know, I was in a hotel room across the state working up the courage to testify in front of a jury in the morning.

Character Witness

All eyes were on me as I walked into the courtroom alone and up to the witness stand. I was trembling hysterically and nearly having a panic attack as the defense attorney stepped up to question me. Flashbacks of the deposition kept popping up. All I wanted to do was crawl under the witness stand and never come out. Recognizing my high stress level, the court took a recess so that I was able to pull myself together and head back out to the witness stand.

This time around, the defense attorney was nowhere near as brutal as he had been to me during the earlier deposition. If he had behaved this way the first time around, I may not have fallen on the bathroom floor of the courthouse. I made it through my testimony and then eagerly waited to meet the other victim.

As promised, I got to meet her that afternoon. She was such a beautiful soul. There were many parallels in our life paths and our aspirations. It was the feeling of meeting an old friend you hadn't seen in years and picking up right where you left off. Except we had never met before, and the only thing connecting us would be one of the most traumatic experiences of our lives.

I wanted to break down and tell her I was sorry. Indeed, I was deeply sorry for not reporting him soon enough. I was sorry she, too, had been raped. I was sorry my wimpy self hadn't been able get the words together to spare other women the wrath of his penis. All I could do was cry, however. The words did not know how to come out.

The day after I testified, the other victim and I stood outside of the courtroom with her family waiting to see more of the trial unfold. The attorney did not want us to walk in together as it might skew the jury's perspective of the victims. She walked in with her whole family as I waited outside the courtroom alone.

After a few minutes passed, I was able to walk into the packed courtroom by myself. This was for sure the loneliest time in my life. I sat in a back pew alone with a heart-shaped rock from the victim advocate. Tears were streaming down my face, as I wondered why my own support system was not there. A rock didn't really fill the void of the support I needed at this time. Listening to the defense attorney tell the jury, "Miss McDaniel laid on her back to receive him" made me burst into tears. I wanted nothing more than to disappear.

When it was time for the verdict, the court let the other victim and I sit together. The jury announced they found him guilty!!! She and I hugged in pure victory. Justice would be served. *Right*?!

In true Melissa fashion, I drove home and went on with life. My coworkers, friends, and most of my family had no clue I was away at a trial.

Life Went On

Once I completed my transfer degree at the community college, I then went to a different University to complete my bachelor's degree. School was my saving grace. My grades reflected how the legal and healing process were fairing. It was painful for me to see my transcript because I knew my potential was greater than the grades I was producing.

My life was on autopilot. Never fully present, I went through the motions to keep me afloat.

Nightmares and anxiety kept me awake at night for fear of being harmed if I fell asleep. When attending university, I took naps in my car between classes because it felt safer to sleep in the daylight than in my own bed at night. If it was winter, I often fell asleep on the benches at the student union building because it was warm and the sound of other people around made it feel comforting and safe.

Looking back now, I find it odd nobody ever stopped to ask if I was okay. Nobody saw through my mask to see if they could help me. Either I am a really great actress, or we as a society are unable to recognize when others are crying out for help.

After the legal process and nearing the end of my bachelor's degree, I set out on mission of desperation to find meaning and purpose again in this thing we called life. Going to Africa had always been on my bucket list. There was no better time than now. Tanzania called my name, and I booked a three-month internship to finish the final quarter of my bachelor's degree.

Here We Go Again

A few weeks prior to leaving for Tanzania, I remember walking through the shopping mall and receiving a phone call. It was the attorneys notifying me the rapist's church and family paid for an attorney to appeal his case. He won the appeal, and the verdict had been overturned.

I sat down at a bench in stunned disbelief. Once I caught my breath, I walked back to my car as fast as I could, tears bursting out of my eyes. We were going to have to do the whole legal process over again. *This has to be a sick joke,* I thought. But it wasn't. It was real, and it was my life.

There was no way I would give up my opportunity to go to Tanzania. He had already taken so much from me. I begged the attorneys not to contact me while I was there and let them know I would tend to my obligations when I returned. My journey to start life over in Tanzania became a short break before returning to the seemingly never-ending trauma.

While in Tanzania, I learned there is so much beauty in meaningful relationships and healing can happen. Spending time with the Tanzanian spiritual healer, the Jipe Moyo mamas, and the other interns brought life back into this broken-hearted woman. I would go as far as saying Tanzania saved my life. This is where the word "acknowledgement" became a staple in my healing process and the first step in the work I do to support women in building meaningful relationships after sexual assault.

When I returned from Tanzania, I learned there was not going to be a trial. Instead, they had been able to reach a plea bargain. *Bittersweet*. He now faced the charge of rape in the third degree with a tremendously shorter amount of time to be spent in prison. This outcome made me lose faith in our judicial system and validated my counselor's past comment that reporting a rape may make life worse for the victim.

Try Again

About six months after graduation and a few months after the final sentencing, I headed for the island of Skopelos, Greece. Some called it running from my problems, but I am here to clarify I was running to something greater than I could have imagined. Greece is where I learned self-love exists and is a powerful thing.

Dancing in tavernas and soaking up the Greek sunshine, I found a new appreciation for myself and "embraced change." The only person in the entire world that I can change is me. If I wanted to begin building meaningful relationships with others, then I needed to take a real look into my life and what was causing the problem. This is the second step that I use when working with other women. We work on embracing the changes that need to occur and love those changes as they help the individual shift into a new way of living.

My graduate studies in holistic leadership helped bring my healing after the sexual assault full circle. It was here I learned about the connection between my mind, spirit, and body and how each plays an integral role in healing. The magic truly happened as they began to work together.

Looking Back to Move Forward

Let's go back to my own lackluster response to the rapist that unfortunate night in May. Although my response is still a mystery to me, the response absolutely saved my life. There are currently five women and one minor who have reported the terror this man has inflicted on their lives in multiple ways. He has spent stints in prison, prior to raping me and after. With this being said, the pain he inflicted will never fully go away. However, through my healing journey after the sexual assault, I have learned how to build meaningful relationships again. This transformative process is a gift bigger than I could ask for. The love for others and myself that I have found at this point far surpasses the disaster that he tried to turn my life into.

He no longer has the power to take away my friendships, partners, and family. The road is not always easy, but the *Beautiful Box of Tools* I have created makes the journey less painful. It has empowered me personally and professionally as I strive to help others through their own journeys after being assaulted.

Chapter 2
Beautiful Box of Tools

T o the woman ready to build meaningful relationships after sexual assault, this *Beautiful Box of Tools* is for you. Within the box you will find the holistic steps used by myself and many other women to move beyond a life of loneliness and isolation and into a life of abundant relationships. Although the first two steps, acknowledge with love and embrace change must be completed in order, the remaining steps are designed to work interchangeably, dependent on where you are in your healing journey.

The framework for the *Beautiful Box of Tools* begins below. I invite you to approach it with a loving mind and curiosity.

Acknowledge with Love

Looking up at the peak of Mt. Kilimanjaro, the Tanzanian spiritual healer spoke his truth while shedding light on mine. Struggling to make sense of life, I desperately needed answers and thought that he would hold the key.

The healer had answers, but they were not the ones I wanted to hear. There was no delicious fruit I could eat and no magic spell; instead, the answer, he said, was within me. Somewhat angry and intrigued, I remember thinking, "How can the answer be within me? Have you seen what's in there?"

He used a beautiful analogy of a radiant flower and honeybees to emphasize his point. At this time in my life, I found the analogy beautiful, but did not understand its meaning. It wasn't until later in my adventure that I learned how important the flower and honeybees would be in moving forward in my journey toward build meaningful relationships.

I believe acknowledging that sexual assault is affecting your ability to build meaningful relationships is the most important and difficult of all the healing steps. For me, there was a big dark cloud following me around for years. I tried to run from it, cut it off, blow it away. Nothing worked. Well, nothing worked until I finally acknowledged it was there. At first, all I could offer it was a distant wave to say hello. Once I finally greeted the cloud, however, magic began to happen.

Although this step is difficult, I encourage you to bear with me. Even if the acknowledgement is only recognizing a fragment of the big dark cloud, that recognition, my dear reader, is growth.

Embrace Change

Waving to the big dark cloud and acknowledging its existence made me extremely aware that it was there, but this awareness alone did nothing to make it float away. Frustrated and wanting relief, I went in search of more answers. With the cloud in tow, I hopped on planes, taxis, and water ferries to the Greek isle of Skopelos. I wish I could say the cloud floated above me like a badge of honor; instead, it was like the heaviest burden I ever have had to bear. My inner voice just kept telling me the word, "change."

I was unsure what the change would look like or how it would feel. All I knew is that it had to happen. Freedom only came once I gave myself permission to embrace change.

Change is never easy. I wish that I could say Greece had the magic spell to relieve me from the presence of the lingering cloud. If it did, I would be handing the magic out like candy. Instead, it gave me something better, the ability to question the kind of love I had for myself.

During this step, I will share my own experience in embracing change and hold the space for you to be able to embrace change in whatever way your heart is called to.

Brilliant Mind

Thoughts of self-hate and disgust continued to hang out in the big dark cloud. Self-love is where I thought I needed to start. Those words were used loosely in my own mind. I chose to only love the parts not associated with the sexual assault. My adventurous soul was the first piece to love because it rarely led me astray. The list of things I loved continued to grow but always excluded the pieces of me that hurt from the sexual assault.

The mind is where I built my two separate lives and held beliefs helping me to walk through life. Questioning my relationship with the mind felt odd at first, but once I got into the groove, it held immense power. The thoughts I held about myself mind, body, and spirit were literally killing me. I was my own worst enemy.

Life began to take flight, when I realized I am not worthless and have immense value in this world. As I owned the cloud's presence as part of me, its color began to slowly add beautiful lavender purple to its distinctly dark shade. *See you later, dark and stink. We are now the color of a light bruise. I'll take it.*

This step will lead you on a journey to question your ways of thinking and support you in deciding if they are serving you well. It will propel you forward into building meaningful relationships with yourself and others.

Sweet Spirit

The damage caused to a person's spirit after sexual assault is often hard to put into words. My spirit felt lost, nowhere to be found. I hung my head often, wondering if there was any point to life. As a young girl, I had always been very spirited. My six-year-old self could be found doing prayer dances on top of her strawberry patch. Why? Because her sweet spirit told her to do so, of course. From a young age, I questioned organized religion and tried to find meaning on my own, hence the strawberry prayer dances. Little Melissa was the coolest. Sadly, she seemed long gone after being sexually assaulted.

While giving my impact statement to the judge, I remember seeing the rapist's pastor sitting in the pew to offer his support to the predator. My sister, Chelsey, friend, Julie, and I looked over at him in disbelief. This was one of those WTF moments.

There was no way I was going to find peace in the Lord after that. At this time, I did not have an organized religion I followed because they never aligned with my core. However, I still did not understand there could be a difference between religion and spirituality. Growing up in a very conservative community, there was little room for interpretation about religion and spirituality. They are one, end of story.

Studying holistic leadership opened my eyes to a whole new ideology of thinking and helped me understand religion and spirituality are not both/and. Their relationship is more of an either/or/and. It is a continuum of love and open to the individual for interpretation. *Hallelujah!*

My sweet spirit began to sing. I now had permission to make meaning in my own way and did not have to be associated with the rapist's belief system. *What? Mind blown.*

This step will support you on the path in connecting with your spirit in a way that makes the most sense for you. You will begin to recognize your sweet spirit has been there all along and is ready to guide you as you reach out to make meaningful relationships.

Rockin' Body

The body is a magical thing. It holds the answers to many of our internal questions and carries us through life like a suit of armor. It is there for your laughter, tears, and happy dances. For me, there were many days I wanted to escape my body. I felt like a spirit trapped inside a dumpster of a bod. *Yuck!*

Body shaming was my go-to defense mechanism. The indescribable pain I felt would often be projected onto my body because my physical parts were easier to name. As I cried on the kitchen floor, I would often blame my fat stomach for being ugly or the cellulite on my legs for not attracting the right men. It was easier to trash what was in front of me when I looked in the mirror than to learn where the pain was actually stemming from. Learning to listen to and connect with my body has been the greatest gift of my life, a gift I cannot wait to share with you.

I had to awkwardly dance in my underwear and color with kid markers to learn to communicate with my body. Let me tell you about how I view this rockin' bod now. My big, strong legs carried me to the witness stand multiple times. My gorgeous blue-green eyes let me shed the tears necessary to see the big black cloud in new colors. Oh and this heart, it kept steadily beating as the rest of me seemed to crash over and over again.

This step may seem odd to you, but I promise you the grace and kindness it brings into your life is very much worth it. The love you have for your body on the inside begins to shine brightly on the outside, attracting the meaningful relationships that you crave.

Beautifully Whole

Sexual assault affects every area of your life, especially when it comes to building meaningful relationships. It can affect your mind and the beliefs you hold about your worth and value. The spirit feels shattered, like the pieces can never be put back together. Your beautiful body becomes a home for self-hate, disgust, and shame. Holding the space for each of those areas to be able to heal individually is mighty powerful. As those pieces start to heal, you can begin to recognize how they communicate together.

Typically, I began to feel something is triggering me by my body's reaction. If my body is showing that it needs some extra love, I call on my mind and spirit to dig into my beautiful toolbox and help find the tool necessary. That tool is then offered with tremendous love to my body.

The communication between my mind, spirit and body is incredible to experience as the conversations unfold. Sometimes, they argue, and other times they are best friends. They need each other. Without one, I am not complete. They make me beautifully whole.

The mind, spirit, and body connection is analogous with the meaningful relationships that we so crave after sexual assault. By connecting to yourself and building the beautiful box of tools for your mind, spirit, and body to connect, you will begin to shine a bright light that works at attracting meaningful relationships.

If the Magic Seems to Fade

Although the *Beautiful Box of Tools* is full of magical resources and healing modalities it is important to mention, obstacles will arise. Occasionally the pain can sneak up on you and the magic will seem fade. In this chapter, you will learn there are multiple ways to rewrite your story. In rewriting your story, you will start to sing a different tune as you find the ability to recognize:

- *You have a beautiful body ready to be loved and respected, not only by yourself, but also by others.*
- *You have a brilliant mind capable of ditching those beliefs not serving you.*
- *You have a fierce inner voice (spirit) ready to speak up and share its deepest fears and desires.*
- *You have amazingly kind people in this world ready and waiting to love you. You are so loved!*

Dance with Me

I invite you to take my hand and begin this beautiful dance to healing on an individual and collective level. Now is the time, more than ever, to start the dialogue about life after sexual assault. It is time to start holding the space for each other to dance in our underwear, laugh as we blow snot bubbles, and learn what is no longer serving us. It is my personal mission to support other sexual assault victims in feeling seen, heard, and loved. I want to help you find your inner goddess and let your true authentic self shine. There are meaningful relationships waiting for you!

Chapter 3
Acknowledge with Love

Affirmation: I acknowledge sexual assault is affecting my ability to build meaningful relationships.

"**A**re you going to Moshi or Arusha when you get off the plane?" asked the kind lady in the Amsterdam airport.

"I'm going to Kilimanjaro," I replied.

She smiled and explained the airport was the Kilimanjaro airport, but upon arrival I must be going to one of the nearby cities. *Oh! Really!*

The joke was on me. Yes, I was going to the Kilimanjaro airport, but beyond the airport I had no clue what city was my final destination. *Awesome.*

At this point in my life, I needed to feel something, anything. Most days, my numb body felt dead and lifeless. It was my final quarter of undergraduate studies, and I was not feeling the excitement of university ending. The previous three years were filled with attorneys, heartache, and the inability to connect with people. The only constant was school.

Taking a giant leap of faith, this small town girl booked a quarter-long internship in Tanzania with the hope of leaving the pain of the previous years behind. There was a glimpse of hope in my eyes that I had not seen since before I had been sexually assaulted. Hope grew into excitement as I began sharing my upcoming adventure with others. I had a conversation starter greater than my crummy college grades and rape trials. *Wonderful!*

The flight took off for my greatest adventure, and I was ready for whatever it would bring. Upon arrival at the Kilimanjaro airport, my driver, Simon, stood outside customs with a sign reading **MELISSA**. *Oh, thank god, somebody was here for me and he knows where I am going.*

As he helped me take my luggage to the *dala dala* (van), I remember softly asking, "Simon, are we going to Moshi or Arusha?"

He looked at me with smiling eyes and said, "Moshi."

A sense of relief came over me, as I then knew where in the world I was going. If only the kind lady was still there for me to tell her. Perception was everything at this stage in my life, and I felt foolish for not having had the ability to tell her where I was going. I had to appear as if everything was together; the slightest sidestep would result in somebody knowing that I hurt deeply.

Simon dropped me off at my home base where I met the most wonderful Mama Grace and other interns from around the world. I felt relief; none of these strangers knew my story. It was pure bliss as I began a fresh start with my new acquaintances.

Having no experience or idea on how to lead a women's empowerment group, I eagerly began my internship with *Jipe Moyo. Jipe Moyo* translates to "take heart, take courage" in English. My time with the group was spent teaching English, leading business meetings, leading support group meetings, working on expanding the chicken project, raising awareness of HIV/AIDS prevention, and conducting weekly home visits. My servant leadership heart was lit with joy as I thought my time with the group would be spent helping them. *Ha*, once again the joke was on me.

Although all of my responsibilities were a great distraction from my life back home, the women there were able to see right through me. Tanzania is a very collective culture. For the most part, everything is about the community and family.

One of the women took one look in my eyes and was able to see the sadness.

I did not have to say a word. My mind was blown. I spent years sleeping in my car and coming to class a hot mess and nobody had said a word. It took only one day in Tanzania, and my secrets were already being brought to light. To me, this meant that I needed to work harder at hiding my secret and the masks needed to be layered on more precisely.

Quickly, the relationships with fellow interns and volunteers went from acquaintances to friends. We danced at *shaki shaki*, laughed as we walked down the streets of Moshi being called *mzungus* (white people), and ate ice cream at Deli Chez. This was my best life: friends, ice cream, and helping others.

We were a few weeks into our internships when my *dadas* (Swahili for sisters) Carly and Doc Daver invited me to join them for a visit with the Tanzanian spiritual healer. Carly was from London, but volunteering in Tanzania during her gap year. Doc Daver was from New Jersey and was there to intern at the local hospital. They were two of the most beautiful souls I have ever met.

Embracing our skepticism, we fearlessly jumped into the white safari truck, ready to gain insight from the healer's sage wisdom. With Kilimanjaro in the distance and bongo flava blasting on the radio, life was nothing short of magical. We giggled as the truck went over boulders in the road, causing our heads to bump into each other in the backseat.

The spiritual healer gave us a tour of his garden, naming off plants and the significance each of them held. He then asked us to find a place in the garden we were drawn to, take a seat, and wait until he was ready.

The healer found me sitting on a rock looking up at Mt. Kilimanjaro and immediately began analyzing the direction I faced. With a stick he drew a compass in the sand. "Northeast," he exclaimed. He then began to paint a beautiful picture with his words.

He stated, "Melissa you have been hibernating like the bears in the north. Almost like you are hiding from the pain 'the man' caused you. But now you are ready to shine your light, like the sun rising in the east."

Whoa, whoa, whoa…who told him about the man and how did this healer know that I was hiding? I could not mask anything in Tanzania.

Not saying a word, I let him continue to paint the picture with his words: "You are like a radiant flower, and every bee is drawn to the color of your flower. You radiate a unique aura. Individuals come near you with the hope to become a part of this aura or with hope of destroying it, making it hard for you to differentiate between the good and the bad people coming into your path. Your aura resembles pollen."

He then went rambling on about me needing to learn to change the color of my flower to heal areas of my life.

Awesome. Next, he had to deliver the answer, right?! "Mr. Spiritual Healer, how do I change the color of my flower?"

In that moment, his response seemed less than life changing. He basically shared the ideology of self-love and really looking at what had caused my flower to become the color it was. Recognizing my frustration, he then sent me to a shed with beautiful stained glass windows to participate in creative and expressive arts with my *dadas*.

The whole way back to home base I pondered his idea of the flower attracting the bees. It was fun to envision my flower to be a bright red hibiscus and imagine all the people who had come into my life with bee wings buzzing around.

My friends at the home base began to learn more about the secret life of Melissa when I started having nightmares around the anniversary of the rape. For years, in the month of May, I would scream "NO" in my sleep and have terrifying visions of me trying to stop people from raping me. Although Tanzania was magic, it was not magical enough to relieve me from the nightmares. Luckily, the friends I shared bunks with were amazing and embraced me with open arms. No questions were asked. There was no interrogation, unlike with the attorneys, and there was also no blame, and no threatening. It was an uncomfortable but pleasant change to feel held in a judgment-free space of love.

A few weeks and over a dozen journal entries later, I chose not to dwell on the color of my flower any longer and chose to acknowledge something was hindering my ability to build meaningful relationships. *Ouch.* That one hurt. It made me feel as if something was wrong with me on a deeper level—a level I did not understand. Although it hurt, I found a greater sense of peace acknowledging there was something within me attracting little to no meaningful relationships over the course of the past three years. It was the first time I felt in control of part of my journey after the sexual assault.

The *Jipe Moyo* classroom became my home away from home. Each day, we laughed, cried, and broke down barriers for women in the village of Rau. Holding the space for women to dialogue about their sexual experiences and trauma was something I never knew I had the strength to do at twenty-three years of age. Although I did not share my experience of being sexually assaulted, many of the mamas chose to share their experiences with me. Some women questioning their cultural beliefs and longing for answers to residual trauma and pain. Never forcing or pushing my cultural beliefs onto the mamas, I found it amazing to watch them acknowledge how their sexual experiences could be hindering areas of their life, too.

The small classroom we taught in was basically a brick structure with open windows and no door. An orange chicken laid eggs beneath the blackboard. The mother hen peacefully sat each day waiting for her babies to arrive. Each morning my co-intern, Amber, and I checked to see if the chicks had hatched. It seemed as if they would never arrive.

The weeks passed too quickly in Tanzania. On our final day at *Jipe Moyo*, the mamas sang to us traditional Swahili songs and showered us with love. Because English grammar is not my forte, I sang many songs with the mamas to teach them the English language. Many times I sang, "You Are My Sunshine," while holding their babies. To my surprise, for their final farewell song, the women draped us with traditional Tanzanian fabric and sang, "You Are My Sunshine." The tears streaming down my cheeks showed my deep love and appreciation for the time spent with these beautiful strong women. Amber and I went to the blackboard one last time; the chicks had HATCHED! It was officially our time to go.

With heavy hearts, we got into the *dala dala*, leaving our beautiful mamas for, what could be, forever. I cried the whole drive back to the home base. The last thing I wanted was to leave this place that had taught me so much about life and community. Although my ability to build relationships to the deep core like Tanzanians was still lacking, I knew it was something to strive for. Acknowledging that the sexual assault was affecting my ability to build meaningful relationships was one of the greatest gifts I received.

What does this mean for you, dear reader?

Acknowledgement is the first step to deeper healing. It is the first step to move forward in building meaningful relationships and changing the color of your flower. Even if the acknowledgement is a small wave of hello to the pain, keep waving. Eventually the full-on acknowledgement will propel you forward to the next steps in building meaningful relationships.

Although my experience of learning to acknowledge may have taken place in Tanzania, acknowledgement can happen anywhere and at any time—in a tiny studio apartment in New York, a mansion in LA, on the beach in Florida, in a Chicago ally. Acknowledgement is something that comes from within and the geographical location in which it occurs is irrelevant. One important piece to acknowledgement is the power in having someone to hold the space for you to acknowledge. I was fortunate to have my *dadas* to hold me on this journey and the spiritual healer to offer his flower analogy.

Acknowledging that the sexual assault is affecting your ability to build meaningful relationships is the most difficult, yet crucial step. If you are ready to move beyond a life of loneliness and isolation, and into a life of truly meaningful relationships, please know I am here to lovingly hold the space for you.

Chapter 4
Embrace Change

Affirmation: I am ready to embrace change.

University was over, and so were all the legal battles necessary to get the rapist in prison. Now what? Everything constant in my life for the previous three years had come to an end. As crazy as it sounds, I had no clue what my new norm would be. Instead of being so consumed with the busyness of completing school and getting somebody locked up, I now had time to think.

Sitting with myself was the scariest thing of all time. The thoughts in my head were not normal, nor did they seem healthy. I remember driving to work hoping another car would hit me—not because I wanted to die but because I thought somebody would have to care for me. I also thought if I was hit by a car, then I would possibly feel something more easily named. The pain of getting hit by a car was easy to describe.

All you have to say is, "I got hit by a car."

The pain of sexual assault is often not easy to describe and comes with an array of feelings. They were feelings that I did not have the vocabulary for. If I had the ability to tell somebody—a friend, anybody—about how I felt about the feelings after the assault, then maybe it would not hurt as bad. Instead, I kept the hidden treasure to myself. Only the treasure was nothing to be coveted, and it felt more like ugly coal.

Sick and tired of feeling lifeless, I knew it was time for help. For me, help meant getting as far away from my current situation as possible. I needed room to breathe and a new perspective. Greece seemed like the ideal place.

I found an ad on Craigslist looking for someone to care for an elderly American woman for the summer.

"Perfect," I exclaimed.

Immediately, I sent off my resume and cover letter. They had to choose me! Within days, I received an email requesting an interview. Dear reader, please don't tell my mom the next part.

My interview was over Skype. I'm not sure why, but my video was not working, and I could only hear the sweet family's voices. With desperation to get out of the current situation, I chose to disregard the need to see the strangers' faces and move forward with the process. Looking back, *HELLO*, this decision was totally not safe. Within three weeks, I was off to my new life in Skopelos, Greece.

When I left for the island, I remember telling my mom I had this strange feeling of being a soul outside of my own body. I could not explain anything beyond that comment—I just knew something was very off. My body was nothing I cared to look at or like. My soul was broken but appeared to be safer to love out of the two.

I jumped on the plane with an open mind and open heart, knowing that I needed to embrace whatever this journey had to offer. Arriving in Athens was complete culture shock. I had no clue how to speak or read Greek. It did not occur to me to try to learn a few words before I left.

My taxi driver John was a riot. He strongly urged me to fall in love.

"Life means nothing without love," he asserted in perfect English. If only the taxi driver knew at this time in my life, I would not recognize love if it fell right in my lap.

John dropped me off at the Athens bus station with my ticket, which was written in Greek. I had no clue what bus to catch or how to get to Volos, my next destination. Practically in tears, I asked everyone who crossed my path for help. Unfortunately, none of them spoke English. The fear of *WHAT THE HECK have I done, who just goes to Greece?* started to sink in. Finally, I found a kind person who understood my frantic gestures and helped me get onto the right bus.

My grand entrance to Skopelos was made on the Flying Dolphin Ferry. Okay, so maybe the Flying Dolphin was not exactly grand, but for the sake of this being "my adventure" I would like to overexaggerate and think of it as *GRAND! No laughing, please!*

The sun was setting behind us as we pulled into the harbor.

As I lugged my bags onto land, I saw Anna (my boss), Yiannis (her husband), and Konstantinos (their thirteen-year-old-son). They greeted me with open arms and helped to carry my bags to the car. Our first stop was a little Greek taverna. You see, there everything was about Greek food and coffee—neither of which I knew anything about.

I am so thankful the charming family and I were able to talk like we had known each other for years. Nothing was awkward. We all laughed at my lack of knowledge of great food and drinks. We talked about everything under the sun. There was never an annoying silence. You know the kind when you are just getting to know somebody—the room gets silent and you can hear the crickets chirping. Instead, our conversations were continuous, one right after the other.

Soon plates and plates of food started coming from the kitchen. It was a little intimidating. The family explained all of the dishes to me one by one. Knowing I had nothing to lose, I tried a bit of everything. When it came time for me to try the deep-fried-sardine-like-headless fish, I wanted to run and hide. But there was no hiding, I had to be brave; I took a bite, bones and all.

It was quite crunchy and disgusting.

Anyone who knows me knows I LOVE to bake cookies—cowboy cookies to be exact. How ironic was it that my new landlord was also the neighborhood baker? He was a skinny man with grey hair. His appearance did not exactly fit how I would picture an old baker, but this is Greece so bakers may look different.

The first time we met, I was in the market next to his bakery attempting to shop. I could not tell the salt from the sugar or the dish soap from the olive oil. It was quite tragic. So the market owner, the baker, and I walked through the store together. Their little English and my ability to create my own type of sign language got us through the process of getting me a few staple groceries. Laughter filled the little market that morning.

My second encounter with the baker was again filled with laughter. He had to come to my apartment to fix the heater and toilet seat. Between his English and my Greek, we could not communicate at all. So out came my silly little sign language and a big smile. Strangely enough, he participated in the random sign language.

Eventually, after a few minutes of us trying to communicate, he took off with my toilet seat and simply said, "Tomorrow."

What? Tomorrow? I guess my toilet seat will be back tomorrow? Not exactly sure!

Sure enough, tomorrow came and so did my toilet seat. Communication with the baker was still difficult, but this time I could say hello and goodbye in Greek. He seemed quite impressed. Sadly, hello and goodbye are exactly the same word. *One word down, many more to go!*

The first day I met Grandma Jean was a hoot. As I entered her small flat, I could hear her muttering something to Anna (her daughter). It turns out they had been discussing where we were going to go for lunch that day. Grandma Jean had recently gotten her teeth pulled so everything she eats needed to be "mushy."

Anna tried to tell her there would be something soft to eat at the restaurant.

To my surprise, Grandma Jean yelped, "I WILL EAT WHATEVER I WELL PLEASE! THANK YOU VERY MUCH!" From then on, I knew we would be the best of friends.

At lunch that day, they ordered an unbelievable amount of food again. I thought my first dinner in Greece had been an exception. Apparently not: It is the golden rule. When you eat there, you really eat!

The food kept coming and coming. I looked at Yiannis and asked if he was trying to make me fat. It was clearly the wrong question to ask. I got a very long explanation of "The statistics show…the Mediterranean diet is one of the healthiest…"

The one thing from the conversation I found the most important were the words, "Melissa, do you see fat people here?"

The obvious response that had to come from my mouth was "NO."

Yiannis went on to explain that in Greece, people enjoy life. They do not worry so much about fat and skinny. They worry about happiness and enjoyment.

So I decided while in Greece and maybe from there on out, I was going to worry less about fat and skinny, and enjoy life. This was the part of the adventure where I had to ask my mom and sister to mail me bigger pants!

It turns out my name literally translates to "honeybee" in Greek. The locals started to refer to me as their little honeybee. I was buzzing around town trying to find my way. My buzzing was about the only noise the town heard then, given that it slightly resembled a ghost town at the time. The tourists would not start to come until May, which gave me plenty of time to establish strong relationships with the locals.

My flat had no TV or Internet. It made for a lot of quiet alone time. I felt the freedom to process in my own way because I had nobody to talk to or feel awkward about trying to mask my pain from. I began buying every book at the bookstore that was written in English. I threw myself into stories of magic, travel, and healing. Slowly I started to feel life come back into my body. It was not such a distant being anymore.

Easter in Greece is one of the most beautiful things I have ever seen. It is amazing to me, the amount of tradition that is still followed here. Greeks have faith unlike anything I have ever seen. The night before Good Friday, the women of the four main churches in town stay up all night making flower arrangements to represent the bed of Christ. On Good Friday, everyone in the town visits each church to see the beautiful flowers.

My sweet little Greek family took me to the oldest church on the island first. We walked into the main room to admire the flower arrangements that the women had made and to light a prayer candle.

There, we found the priest cleaning the candleholders. He was the cutest man I had ever seen: so short, chubby, and bald. For some reason the chubby little man kept looking at me funny.

He then asked Yianni my name. "Melissa, honeybee."

The typical thing happened. "Her name is Honey bee? Hahaha."

The priest went about his cleaning business for a while and then chuckled, "Melissula!!"

My little host family and I looked at each other. *WHAT?* You see, Melissula was what Anna and Yianni had begun calling me, but they were the only ones on the island who had called me this until that moment. It was a term of endearment they had created.

Having the priest, who I had never met me before and never heard the family call me that then randomly blurt out "Melissula" felt rather odd.

Yianni and the priest started talking in Greek. I obviously had no idea what was going on; my knowledge of the Greek language was still very small.

I was in my own little world, taking in the beauty around me, with prayer candle in hand, and a look of awe on my face. As I lit my prayer candle with the holy flame and placed it in with the other prayers, Yianni looked at me and said, "The priest says you are a TREASURE. He said one look in your eyes, Melissula, and he can see you are a rare and special person."

The statement made me get a little teary eyed. Melissula, the girl who had lost faith in so many things had a priest telling people she was a treasure. You would think the priest could see I was one lost girl and would tell me to go find Jesus or something, not simply say, "Melissula, you are a treasure."

I left the small church feeling strangely seen. It made me believe that there would be deep healing while I was in

Greece, and maybe I would finally be able to feel something other than numbness and pain.

As spring came to an end and the summer was upon us, Skopelos began to come to life. The hustle and bustle of the tourists and the wonderful Greek shops filling with life was a nice change from the boarded-up doors and quiet streets. It was funny how we both began to blossom together.

I'm very much a kinesthetic processor—meaning that for me, my ability to heal and learn happens best when my body is moving. In each place I live or travel to, I have a thinking spot that is only magical if walked to. Greece was no exception.

While hiking to my thinking spot, the words of the Tanzanian spiritual healer came rushing back to me. The need to change the color of my flower and the ideology of self-love were at the forefront of my brain. *Hmm.*

Feeling a bit goofy, I started saying, "Honeybees, flowers, self-love…what is happening?"

Then it hit me, right in the face: My name legit means honeybee. Maybe if this honeybee learns to love herself, the color of her flower will change. *What? If I fully accept myself, imperfections and all, I can begin to heal this pain.*

Sitting in my thinking spot trying to process the magic that just happened, I cried. It took me flying all the way to Greece to have this epiphany. It took a Tanzanian spiritual healer and learning my Greek name to recognize the way in which I viewed the color of my flower (myself) was hindering my ability to progress forward and build meaningful relationships. And in that moment, I knew it was time to embrace change. It was time to look my flower right in its center and learn to see it in a new light. The only problem was I had no clue how.

I felt a bit guilty for originally thinking the Tanzanian spiritual healer's advice on self-love had been "less than life changing." His advice was everything. I just hadn't been in a place to receive the message. By beginning with acknowledging the sexual assault was affecting my ability to build meaningful relationships, I was now able to see things in a different light. This light then led me to recognizing the only way to move forward in the healing process was to learn to love myself and embrace the changes that needed to occur, including the idea of changing the color of my flower.

The next step for you, dear reader, in beginning to build meaningful relationships after sexual assault is to embrace change needs to happen. This does not mean external change, but the change must come from within you.

While in Greece, I did not have the vocabulary to verbalize what areas I needed to embrace change. However, I knew it needed to happen. Just like recognizing I needed to acknowledge how my relationships were being affected, embracing change gave me the freedom to know my life does not have to continue down the same path I've been walking.

I encourage you to go out for an intentional walk and move your beautiful body. Set the intention to really listen to your inner voice and discover in what areas of your life may need to embrace change in order for you to build meaningful relationships. When you return home, hold your thoughts with love and journal.

Chapter 5
Brilliant Mind

*Affirmation: I have the power to change
my life, by changing my thoughts.*

The thoughts you carry, day in and day out, shape your reality and help you to make sense of the world. They can carry you through life with grace and compassion or can inflict the worst pain. It was not until I started studying holistic leadership that I realized the importance of having a relationship with my mind. The beliefs we carry are stored because we were told by others, "This is how you should think," and/or the ideas were developed as you tried to make sense of the world. Did you know you have the power to change your thoughts and beliefs? If you are willing to step outside the box you have built yourself into, life can begin to transform.

After being raped, I held many unique beliefs about myself and how to navigate the world. To deter others from recognizing my pain, I always had a conversation starter to shock, awe, and make them giggle. The first story I typically told to new acquaintances was about my adventures of taking pigs to the county fair.

Many times, this conversation would lead into the process of preparing one's pig for the fair, how to get them to stop and turn with the simple touch of a cane, and what type of pig butt the judges were looking for. You read that right, pig butt! This silly banter could go on for at least thirty minutes.

It was a great way to deter the conversation from anything important. If this effort did not get a giggle, there were plenty of other stories to veer us away from any thoughts of thinking or feeling. If I had to see people a second time, I would make sure to have another conversation starter prepared.

I would talk about things like the summers I participated in Grandma School. My cousins and I marched around the alfalfa field with batons while learning to twirl like show girls. We rode the four-wheelers to pick pie cherries and then bake the tastiest mini pies in the world.

"God Bless America" was Grandma's song of choice. I still giggle every time I hear my little sister Chelsey's squeaky voice singing, "WHITE WITH FOAM!" As children, we sang for nursing homes, the next-door neighbors, and poor Grandpa over a million times.

If the country bumpkin stories did not make the cut, I always had my adventures to Tanzania and Greece to fall back on. The time Chelsey and I took an overnight ferry from Greece to Italy always gives people a good laugh. In that adventure, we turned on country music on the deck and taught our fun new Greek friends how to country dance at 1 a.m.

I like to call these my comedic conversations. They made me feel funny, valued, and like I had something to contribute to our conversations. However, things always got tricky once I ran out of comedic things to say. The rest of my life was not as exciting as cherry pies and Porkahontas.

This point is at which I began to fumble. I would push people away or flat out run. I began to live two separate lives. This idea was true for both friendships and dating relationships. If my newfound friend really knew how weak I was inside, would she truly want to hang out with me? My new partner could never love me if he knew my truest thoughts.

In one of my many failed attempts at dating, I will never forget when my boyfriend said something along the lines of this: "My dad told me I needed to really make sure you are worth it because I am going to have to live with you being raped for the rest of my life, too."

I was horrified and heartbroken. Was being raped such a negative thing a father felt he had to step in to coach his son on whether or not I was worth it? This moment is when I started to form beliefs about my worth in a relationship. What I had going on was too much of a burden for another to bear, let a lone want to be with me. I carried this belief for years. I began to sexualize myself. If a guy was not going to want me because I had been raped, maybe I just needed to be a little sexier and prettier. My worth became based on my external offerings rather than my internal self.

The relationships I attracted into my life were horrible. Don't get me wrong. There have been some wonderful friends and partners who have come into my life, but the majority of those whom I attract treated me the same way I treated myself. *Wait, what?* Yep, I said it right.

The relationships I attracted mirrored the beliefs and feelings I had about myself. In my head, I was never thin enough, never pretty enough, never smart enough, and never worth enough to have authentic love or friendships.

I also carried around the big, forbidden label: rape victim. *Cringe.* The beliefs I held were a big contributor to me living those two separate lives. The world saw the cool, confident Melissa who was overly educated and well traveled; she had friends all over the world and not a care in the world. The other was crying behind closed doors because the indescribable pain she felt was sometimes too much to handle.

The *aha* moment happened when I learned there are beliefs in our lives that serve a great purpose. Although they may have been serving a great purpose, sometimes they no longer serve in your best interest.

In one of my leadership classes, I remember the faculty member handing out a piece of yarn to each student and asking us to create a circular boundary. The only criterion was it had to be big enough for us to sit in. I carefully crafted mine into a spiral with a great, strong outer boundary. This endeavor felt so silly and strange, but I planted my bum right in the middle and waited for our next instruction.

Next, she gave us note cards. On the cards, we had to write about the things in our life serving us well. For example, my brain—it was serving me well in that I have the ability to take graduate-level classes and somewhat process this odd task. Things not serving me well were my inability to speak openly about my real feelings. Each thing serving me well went into the spiral circle with me. The things not serving me well got crumpled and tossed aside.

Gosh, it felt good to throw the trash out of my circle. By the end of the experiential exercise, I was left with a great gift of things serving me well in order to help me on my journey. In true Melissa fashion, I did not let myself dive too deeply into this exercise's deeper meaning because we were in class and heaven forbid that others might see what's really hiding within me. In the coming month, however, this tool became my biggest eye-opener. In many challenges I faced in moving forward after the rape, I was able to sit down with my yarn and decipher what tools were going to help propel me forward.

On one particularly snowy day in Rhode Island, I was confined to my studio apartment and the terrible beliefs I held about my ability to build meaningful relationships. Once again, I had attracted another person who made me feel so small and worthless. Owning change needed to happen, I busted out my green yarn, note cards, and willing heart to have a real meaningful experience with myself.

As I began to write comedic conversations, tears filled my eyes. The conversation starters were no longer serving a purpose. They held the power when I needed them because I was not ready to face myself, but they were no longer holding a positive space in my life. I crumpled up the note card and threw it out of my circle.

Feeling a bit lost, I could literally feel the space in me opening up for a new way of being. The next thing I had to address were my beliefs about my worthiness for meaningful relationships. The belief I carried for so long about others not wanting to be my friend or partner because I had been raped needed to go. A bit unsure about how to release this one, I wrote it in my best English, then crumpled the note card up and threw it as far away possible. In my studio apartment, the paper probably only made it somewhere near my mini stove. Nonetheless, it was out of my circle and made room for new beliefs.

I continued on with this exercise for an hour—with me tossing out words like *I'm ugly, broken, and worthless.* Then I began adding things in to my circle like, *I'm beautiful* (not in a sexualized way) *I'm worth meaningful, kind relationships*, etc.

As I owned my beliefs and the need for them to change, magic began to happen. Releasing those beliefs made room for new, kinder ones. There was freedom in breaking the cycle of my mind. Although this epiphany was magical, there were days the old ways of thinking would creep in. *Nobody will love my damaged body. Ugh.*

How in the world did this dark thinking come back? It took practice—so much practice to retrain my mind. There were days when I tried to work through things, and the pain would not have words associated to it.

When I could not find the words, I was encouraged to visual journal. If anyone has seen my artwork, they know it looks worse than a six-year-old. Nonetheless, owning change needed to happen, I took out my oversized markers and drew every time there were no words. At first, this endeavor proved to be very difficult for me. I am freaking judgmental of myself.

Eventually my mind stopped fighting the process and the pictures started to flow. It gave me a new way to release my thoughts without having to know the exact words to say. For me, the feelings associated with being raped did not always have a word or words. Did it make them any less painful? *Absolutely not.* Visual journaling gave me the tool to connect in a new way.

So there I was, a grown woman sitting in a nest of yarn with her markers and begging to live her best life. I could feel real healing begin to happen. I began to notice the wonderful, beautiful friends popping into my life. Some had been there all along, and I was finally able to recognize their presence. Others were new, budding relationships with so much potential.

The comedic conversations did not totally disappear. Who doesn't like a good pig story, right? But I felt freedom in opening myself up in a new way to people. No, this change did not mean dishing my whole life story to the world. It did, however, mean putting FAR less energy in trying to control every conversation and more into letting the conversations develop naturally.

I chose not to live two lives any longer. It's exhausting trying to be two people. I still did not quite know how to own my story, but I knew this newfound connection with my mind was leading me to my next great relationship—my relationship with spirit.

If you would like a free copy of the yarn experiential exercise instructions or visual journaling prompts please email me at melissa@lovemelissaann.com.

Chapter 6
Sweet Spirit

Affirmation: I trust my sweet spirit.

I t was the night before I had to read my impact statement to the judge. My sister, Chelsey, and friend Julie sat with me as I prepared the statement. Their strength and encouragement helped me fight through the tears to write something halfway coherent. I don't think I slept more than an hour over the course of the night. Nerves and a monster cold sore were the bane of my existence.

The ladies and I woke up early and quietly prepared for what felt like the worst thing we could be doing on the gloomy day. As we made our way to the courthouse, I remember wishing and praying not to run into the rapist's family at the security check. One look at them and my whole body would go into a state of panic. With Chelsey and Julie by my side, we entered the courtroom ready to take on whatever may come our way.

When it was time to read my impact statement, Chelsey and I walked hand in hand up to the judge with tears in our eyes. The rapist to my right and his family in the pews made this walk extremely intimidating.

My impact statement was read as a tearful mumble. I spoke of having to relocate to a new town and transfer schools. I spoke of begging attorneys not to reach out to me while I was in Tanzania. Of all the things I spoke of, the one that hurt the most was the damage to my spirit. I explained how the rape had impacted every piece of what makes Melissa, Melissa. It made life unbearable at times.

As Chelsey and I walked back to our seats, we noticed the rapist's pastor sitting in the pews. He had been at the man's side throughout the whole journey, even funding the appeal. Although it isn't very godly, I remember wanting to rip the cross off his neck and shove it down his throat. *What man of god supports a rapist?*

That supposed man of god heard my story multiple times and the stories of others the rapist had inflicted pain on. He saw me almost crawl under the witness stand as I testified in front of a large jury. He watched me run sobbing out of the courtroom because the sight of the defense attorney made me have a panic attack. *Who was this guy?*

The deputies were concerned for our safety and escorted us out of town by police car. I felt like my life was the movies again. *Who gets escorted by police car?*

I appreciated their concern for our safety and the respectful manner they treated us with. We turned on "Not Ready to Make Nice" by the Dixie Chicks again and drove as fast as we could out of the town. It was over, officially this time.

Growing up in a small conservative town, there were very few options to explore religion and spirituality other than the multiple forms of Christian churches. Organized religion was spirituality to me; my young mind had no other way of understanding the two. At the age of four, I asked my grandmother, "How did the three wise men know which star to follow to find Jesus?" Stumped, she changed the subject.

I found comfort in knowing there was a higher being, but I was unsure if the stories from the Bible resonated with me. My sweet little girl spirit was always standing on top of my strawberry patch doing prayer dances to a goddess. I do not know who the goddess was, but I sure loved to choreograph prayer dances in her honor. It makes sense now as to why some of my family members called me a flower child. Little Melissa was a flower goddess!

Being sexually assaulted created a dissonance from anything religion or spiritual related. My spirit was shattered! The beliefs I clung to about religion and spirituality were not supporting me to move forward in healing.

As I dove into the studies of holistic leadership, I quickly learned religion and spirituality do not have a both/and relationship. They can operate congruently or as separate beliefs. *What a relief.* I did not have to find meaning the way the pastor did. I could make meaning my own way.

I began to immerse myself in different modalities of connecting to spirit. Quickly, I learned the spirit I was searching for had been with me all along this journey. I didn't have a name for it, but it was definitely there. The little inner voice telling me to go to Tanzania: spirit. The boisterous voice telling me to go to Greece: spirit.

My biggest eye-opening encounter with that sweet spirit was when it called me to go to Salve Regina University. I had never been to the campus; in fact, I had never been to Rhode Island. Something about the photos of the majestic campus told me it was the place for me.

With the intention of being admitted into school, I sold everything I owned, except what would fit in my two-door Honda Civic. I had a studio apartment to view upon my arrival and a job interview lined up. There was no other plan but to succeed.

I drove across country with my sleeping destinations mapped out and no other care in the world. It was liberating, knowing I was doing it, freaking doing it. Whatever "it" was felt fantastic.

I laughed and cried the whole way to Rhode Island. There were moments of hysterics as I dealt with the pain coming forward in the silent car. There were giggles with the random people who saw my car filled with garbage bags. Yes, I'm so high class I packed my stuff in trash bags. It made my stuff more malleable and gave me the ability to stuff more in the car. *Genius really!*

Within five days of my arrival in Rhode Island, I had a place to live and a job. I went to the campus, in awe of its historical beauty, and slowly walked to the admissions office. My fate was in their hands. I nervously asked if the office had received my transcripts from my previous graduate school. The admissions counselor pulled up my file and said something along the lines of, "Yes. Oh and by the way, you have already been admitted to the program."

I held back the happy tears and dancing until I left her office. Dashing as fast as I could to the Newport Cliff Walk, tears of pure happiness fell from my cheeks. It worked. It freaking worked. Trusting in whatever was telling me to go and not look back was and still is the best thing I could have done on my journey to learn how to build meaningful relationships after the rape.

In my first quarter at Salve, I remember a wise professor telling me, "Melissa, you have to do the work."

Not quite understanding the full meaning of her statement at the time, I still fully immersed myself in the work—whatever it might be in the moment. As I learned about the continuum of spirituality and religion, and let my old mental model shift, the sweet spirit I once had came flooding back.

Many times, spirit has a different connotation for everyone. Some may refer to spirit as god, goddess, a higher power, love; the list is endless. Some may even call it intuition. My definition is ever growing. For right now, I believe there is a higher power; I also believe the higher power is connected to me. We are one. God is in me and around me. Spirit is love, and the love is not defined by any one particular god. I find beauty in all religion and the meaning and purpose it provides to others.

I have meditated with monks, danced with the Maasai, and Opa'd with Greeks. Each experience equally connects to spirit in the way that it resonates with them. *Beautiful!*

My newfound love for spirit had me meditating for deeper connection. The journeys meditation took me on were like a mini vacation from my negative ways of thinking. Those journeys also helped me build a deeper connection with my mind. The beliefs that were no longer serving me took what seemed to be forever to transform. Meditation helped me work through and make meaning in new ways.

I also began to feel a greater sense of being able to connect to my core. My ability to trust myself was long gone after the rape. Everyone was bad and could not be trusted. The more I learned to trust my spirit and my natural instincts to know what feels right (to me), the less problem I had with building meaningful relationships. It was not easy, but I let myself kind of play with the idea of trusting my higher self/spirit in safe spaces. When building relationships with classmates, I would try to feel the vibe and see whom I could and could not disclose my feelings to. Ninety percent of the time my spirit was spot on. *Wow!* The other ten percent happened when I let my mind and negative thoughts take over. Ninety/ten is a huge improvement from zero percent.

When the pain becomes hard, which sometimes it still does, I now know to trust my spirit. If it guides me to do a guided meditation, I meditate. If it tells me to go for a walk by the river, I walk. If it tells me to just sit on the floor and cry, I cry. I do not doubt my spirit and its ability to help me heal when I need it. The relationships it shares with my mind are so complimentary. If I begin to overthink myself into tears, my spirit comes in to support me in knowing how to help myself—and vice versa. If I begin to doubt my spirit, I have my mind to whisper to me: trust.

There is no one right way to build a relationship with your sweet spirit. However, I encourage you to sample some of the tools listed below:

- **Guided Meditation**: Email me at melissa@ lovemelissaann.com and we can create one together.

- **<u>Visual Journaling</u>**: When you find that your spirit wants to communicate and you are not finding the words to do so, turn to expressive art. Let go of perfection and draw, color, paint. Whatever moves you, do that!

- **<u>Intentionally Walking</u>**: If you too are a kinesthetic processor, go out for an intentional walk to communicate with your spirit. Let nature guide you and bring your sweet spirit to life.

Although the two—mind and spirit—work beautifully together, I found something was still missing. It was the part of me I most dreaded connecting to: my body. *Ugh.*

I encourage you to continue on this journey with me and to do the work. It will not lead you astray.

Chapter 7
Rockin' Body

Affirmation: My body has value and
purpose in the world. I love my body.

A s I looked out at the beautiful blue Aegean Sea, tears filled my eyes as I recollected memories from the night before. Nothing terribly tragic happened. I just felt stupid— one minute I was dancing with my friends at the club, and the next minute I had no clue how to be in relation with other humans. On this particular night, I cried myself home after a few too many glasses of red wine, feeling embarrassed.

Embarrassed for what? I'm not sure. My mind would immediately go to blaming my body for not dancing well enough or my voice for not knowing the right thing to say to newfound friends. This was a common occurrence when I tried to build relationships. Comedic conversations only lasted so long, and then I had to be real. Real was scary. Real meant demonstrating authenticity and transparency, neither of which I was ready to do.

Prior to being raped, I had been a very confident young woman. I never viewed my body as perfection, but I also didn't despise its existence. After being raped, my body was nothing to me. I avoided looking at it in the mirror and chose to speak pure hatred to my curves.

Blame was placed on my body for being too sexy or my boobs for being too big. Clearly, it had to be its fault he raped me. The parts of my body were easy to name. They were tangible, unlike the feelings and the shame I felt.

While holding hatred on the inside, the outside appeared to be an overly confident woman without a care in the world. The more I tried to appear as a confident young woman, the more my ego would take over and tell me, *I'm worthless.*

I began to sexualize my body. Ultimately, sex was the only thing it was good for. Sure, sex could be fun, but it had no meaning. I found myself in sexual situations saying, "yes" because I was scared to say "no." If I gave consent, there was no harm done; he didn't rape me. The way I viewed my body and its relationship to sex was very counterproductive.

My mind would often say, "You and your stupid curvy body are attracting men like a whore."

But the presumably unwanted attention also stroked my ego and fed into my beliefs about external self-worth.

The reality of this counterproductive belief system set in in Greece. Something was off, and I was starting to acknowledge my body might be communicating. Now, I was really losing it. *How can my body talk?* The feeling of being a soul outside a body was more prevalent than ever. My numb body did not know how to recognize the simplest pleasures. *Get your mind out of the gutter,* if it went there. This disconnect meant not recognizing the joy to be had at everything from grooving on the dance floor to feeling the sand between my toes.

I am a dancer, albeit not in the sense of a classically trained dancer; I'm more like a two-year-old in a tutu. Nonetheless, I love to dance and so do Greeks. There were days when my whole body would feel the music. And then there were days I noticed my body dancing, except my arms. Seriously, my arms would try to cling to my sides as the rest of me gained rhythm. I'd try to fling them from side to side and up and down. Nothing. They were stuck and not going anywhere.

At this time in my life, all I could do was acknowledge the weirdness of my non-groovy arms and embrace change needed to happen. How silly I must have looked dancing with frozen arms. During my time studying the synthesis between mind and body, the *aha* moment happened.

My frozen arms were trying to speak; I just didn't know how to listen. For one of the class projects, we were asked to create our own movement experiential exercise and practice it for the majority of the semester. Dance was the easiest way for me to relate to movement, so I decided to dance at least three times a week, in front of the mirror, in my underwear.

At first, it was awkward watching my body move to the music. Some days, it made me laugh, and other days it made me feel like a fool. Knowing I needed to, "do the work," I kept dancing. Dancing sad, happy, and somewhere in between, I wrote the outcome of each dance in a journal, choosing to visual journal if I did not understand the words. Just as it was difficult for me to name the words associated with all the feelings I experienced, it was also difficult to understand what my body was communicating. Frozen arms did not seem very meaningful to me at the time.

There were days I played with polarities in dancing, meaning I would make big, grand gestures followed by mindful, small gestures. When my arms chose not to participate, I leaned into the lack of movement and embraced the story they were trying to tell. Looking back, I envision myself dancing similarly to a penguin. I would then dance with big orangutan arm twirls to see how the polarities resonated within me. This seemed to lighten my mood and also gave new meaning to my body and its abilities.

I would then draw how the two polarities expressed themselves. Sometimes they came out as burst of colors, and other times, it was stick figures. On the days my arms did not want to dance, they told me they were scared to reach out to others. Connecting while dancing can be a sacred bond. My body was actually telling me it was scared to bond. What a smart little thing it is.

As my insights grew, so did my exploration with dance. There I was in all my glory and mismatching underwear shaking it like there was no tomorrow. It felt good. The movements my body made while dancing were majestic. My stomach undulated like a belly dancer. My hips shimmied like the Tanzanian mamas. Instead of running from the disgust I typically felt, I started craving what my body had to say and how it wanted to move.

Until one day, it hit me like a ton of bricks, because the aftermath of rape sometimes works like that. You do not know when the pain will hit, but when it does, watch out. You can't miss it. Your body always knows. It is a genius wrapped in skin and sealed with the ability to endure the impossible. The small glimpses of love for my body had been washed away by thoughts of disgust and hatred.

In the usual Melissa meltdown spot, the kitchen sink, I collapsed to the floor in tears. The pain and disgust I felt for myself was completely contradictory to the love I was developing the weeks prior. What was happening? I felt defeated. Glancing over at the mirror propped up on a chair next to my refrigerator, I thought, *"Melissa you should dance."*

My ego kicked in to tell me how stupid I was for dancing and coloring in a visual journal: "*You are a grown woman; get it together and put your markers away.*"

Fighting back the tears, I put on some tunes and stripped down. Only this time, I stripped down bare naked.

So there I was in my birthday suit with a red tomato face, tears streaming down my face and snot coming out my nose. *Clearly not a pretty crier!* All I wanted was to find a small piece of love for this horrendously damaged thing I had to carry around.

My feet felt stuck to the floor like cement and my arms glued to my sides. Instead of running to put on clothes and hide my hideous face, I stood there trying to find one ounce of good. It had to be there. I just knew it.

Once the tears ran out, I began to laugh at myself in the mirror. The laughter loosened up my body, and it began slowly swaying with the music. Eventually my arms started to join in. My ego would start to say, *"Look at the nasty cellulite on those gigantic thighs."* My sweet spirit and mind chimed in together, *"Look at those strong thighs that carried you to the witness stand."* It was like being in a war zone, only this time love had no option but to win. The ego's daggers were sharp, but they were no match for my desire to embrace change and build a new relationship with my body.

We became the best of friends, communicating through movement and dance. If my body reached out for help, I helped. I would have done anything to keep this love alive.

As I listened to my body's pain and joy, I found a new sense of respect. No longer did I feel the need to sexualize myself for validation. Feeling attractive to men was nice, but did not hold the value it previously had done. Sex was no longer just sex and my body was no longer just a vessel to perform the deed. My body has value and purpose in the world. Let's say that one again. My body has value and purpose in the world. There is so much power in those words.

When I finally took the time to listen to the pain and trauma my body endured, it gave me the freedom to heal. The raw communication coming from my body helped me learn to be more authentic in my healing process. As the love and respect grew for myself, my relationships began to flourish. I was able to connect with people on a different level.

Through this process of connecting to my body, I learned movement and creativity are key. If my body calls out for help, I make sure the healing or experiential activity I do has a movement component. It must also offer grace for me to be creative in the process. Drawing the feelings in a visual journal gave me the ability to make meaning out of my body's communication without feeling lost or upset for not understanding. Although I may not know the words, I know exactly how the image resonates with my body.

Just as we used movement to connect with our sweet spirits, I encourage you to use movement to connect with your body. Trauma from sexual assault can leave you feeling paralyzed at times. Hence, my arms: the same arms I used to try and push the predator off of me were the arms scared to reach out and connect with others. Kindly notice how your body is moving around in the world. Do you notice there are times your legs feel jittery and like they need to move? Approach those jittery legs with love and ask them if they want to chat. Go for a walk, run, and/or dance if they are calling you to. Even if you do not know what they are trying to say, by acknowledging their presence they will feel loved. You can visual journal or write a journal entry; there is no right way to communicate. Your body will appreciate you are trying.

The beauty in learning to lovingly communicate with your body also offers you the opportunity to connect with your mind and sweet spirit. Individually they are powerful; when they work together as a whole, this is where the magic happens.

Chapter 8
Beautifully Whole

Affirmation: I am beautifully whole!

When life begins to feel overwhelming, I often find peace in knowing my mind, spirit, and body are great indicators of what I need to heal in the moment. They have a beautiful dance supporting me to live life to the fullest after sexual assault. The struggles I faced in building relationships with partners, friends, and family have started to dissipate.

For years I attracted terrible dating relationships. Typically, I gravitated to men who made me feel less than.

I gravitated to these men because it was exactly how I felt about myself on the inside. They were confirmation of my own mental models.

Exhibit A: When I felt fat and despised my body, I easily found a man to confirm this hatred for me. I went as far as falling madly in love with a man who consistently verbally degraded my body because it did not meet his standard of fit. Even after losing eleven pounds, I still was not physically enough in his eyes. His vision of my imperfect body felt great, because it confirmed everything, I already knew about myself.

Exhibit B: If I felt broken on the inside, you better believe I found a man who crushed those pieces even smaller. I'll never forget the man who threw his open bag of Cheetos across my off-white couch and then proceeded to scream at me as I sat crying in the hallway floor. He screamed because I wanted to talk about my PTSD and how my anxiety was acting up. He felt he didn't have time to talk about this one more time.

Exhibit C: Let's not forget the noncommittal men I gravitated to. I never believed someone would stick around with a woman who had been raped. *Why would they?* I was damaged. So what did I do? I attracted men who did not want to commit. Why? Because it validated my beliefs of not being good enough to be with long term. These were the men who thought I was so *HOT,* but would never commit to a relationship with me. I was an object to them, a piece of ass. *Ah! How messed up.*

When a kind person crossed my path, I ran far, far away. It was easier to run than try to believe I was the beautiful person they saw. I did not have the ability to see myself in the mirror they were holding up. In fact, the reflection coming my way terrified me. If I saw myself as beautiful and with purpose, I would have to throw out all the beliefs I held and create a new life. The thought of a new life seemed impossible.

Friendships were difficult because I tried to lead two separate lives. I had my groups of friends I trusted to know and my group of amazing acquaintances who were forbidden to know. Just as I separated my mind, spirit, and body, I also separated my friends in order to protect my heart.

There were days it felt so good to be held in love by the friends who knew. Then there were days I wish I never told them. It was not because they could not hold the space for me, but because I had to face my pain and be vulnerable.

It was a double-edged sword. I pushed people away that I loved because I did not know how to have conversations about the pain I felt on the inside. Not knowing how to speak with my body, change my mental models, or listen to my spirit made me timid and constantly wanting to fly away. I flitted to and from different states and countries, meeting new friends, just to leave them and begin the journey again.

The relationship with my family was one of the hardest after the sexual assault. I felt as if I was a disappointment and disgrace. Some individuals made me feel this way in the beginning. The comments of: "You let him into your bed and didn't think he would have his way with you?" and "You created this mess," made it difficult to feel as if I had a space in my family. Nobody deserves to be raped. I should be able to walk naked down the street and not get raped. *No, I was not asking for it!* Eventually, my family began to sing a different tune.

Today, they are fiercely supportive and have my back. Many of my family members did not know I was raped; some still do not. When going through the legal process, I was able to count the number who knew on two hands. I didn't even need to use the toes. I hated to attend holiday parties and chose to stay away as often as I could. My biggest fear was that they would see through me and pick up on my pain.

The sweet girl who danced in her strawberry patch was no longer sweet on the inside. She was ugly and disgusting. Comments of being an old maid and "Why are you still single?" hurt to the core. If only they knew I so deeply wanted those things, but I did not know how to attain them after the sexual assault.

As I started to learn the thoughts in my mind shaped my outer world, the *aha* moments began. While my beliefs about my worth and myself began to shift, I found my sweet spirit started speaking to me more. It would share glimpses of who I used to be: the fearless little girl prayer-dancing on top of her strawberry patch to the beautiful goddess within; the young belly dancer that loved every one of her curves and the way they moved in the mirror. As my spirit began to speak up, my body physically started to change its appearance. People began commenting on how much lighter and free I looked. And I was receptive to the feedback. That was a miracle in itself.

While the beauty of each separate part of me began to unfold, the real magic happened when I realized... *Hello, they are all working together, and I am only as strong as my weakest part.* This realization led me on a mission to discover all the beautiful ways my mind, spirit, and body are communicating.

When my mind begins to rabbit trail off into the land of self-hate and disgust, it clearly needs some love. I call on my body and spirit to do so. The dancing in front of the mirror and visual journaling give my body ways to communicate with both my mind and spirit. As I draw and write, the words spoken from my body and my spirit, my mind begins to hum a different tune. With a deep breath, it says, *"Oh that's right, those beautiful legs carried you down this journey, and you are brilliant."* Pure magic.

The communication has become an addiction. It feels so good to feel good again. When my body begins to feel anxious, it knows to trust my mind and spirit to provide the love and support necessary. Anxiety often occurs near the anniversary of the rape. My mind quickly tells me to check my cute buns into counseling. There, I spend time loving my spirit and working through the anxiety.

How does all this information relate to the dating relationships at the beginning of the chapter? Well, let me tell you about my dating life now. The more fiercely I love myself, the more fiercely those I attract love me. The kindness I speak to myself is reflected in the kindness they speak to me. The body I was so ashamed of and had used as a tool to sexualize myself is no longer the object of their affection. Their compliments stem from my beautiful soul and the super smart brain in my head. By loving my body and respecting the magical being that it is, I only surround myself with those who do the same. My tolerance is zero for anyone who does not value the wonderful being that I am.

The family I distanced myself from has slowly started to come back into my life with a deeper love than I have ever known from them. Relationships are being mended and conversations are getting real. Feelings are not held back or hidden: It is real or nothing. There is room for growth, but, my gosh, is it developing beautifully. I no longer want to hide under the table at Thanksgiving or avoid family when I go to my hometown for a visit. The persona of not being a human has been removed, and I let them see the real me.

My insecurities around letting all my friends know when I am in pain have floated away. I let myself live authentically in the moment. No, I do not dish my life story to everyone, but the ones I choose to disclose it to have never once loved me any less. There is so much freedom in living one life filled with all of me. Some individuals have joined in on the funky visual journaling, soul collaging, dancing. We laugh and cry together as things come to the surface.

The connection between my mind, spirit, and body take work, but it the most important work I will ever do. Each part has held me with grace and offered me freedom from my old ways of living. Without building this fierce relationship with myself, I would not be able to build relationships with others. The love and respect with which I hold myself shines a mirror out to the world about the type of relationships I will allow in my life. My body is to be treated like the goddess it is. The curves, cellulite, and big boobs are to be held with the utmost respect.

The hardest part of me to accept was the fact that I was raped. I did not want it to be a piece of me. It floated and lingered around as a looming cloud I could not escape. Blowing it away, trying to cut whatever it was tied to, and imaging it wasn't there, never worked. It was still there.

The minute I embraced being a rape victim was the minute the cloud started to fade. The years I spent running from such a huge part of my life was only hindering my ability to build relationships with others and myself. Owning my story has supported my healing by leaps and bounds.

Originally, I thought labeling myself as a rape victim would be the only definition tied to my name. It turns out I am a rape victim, but it is only a small piece of what makes up me. I am also a sister, daughter, granddaughter, friend, dancer, writer, auntie, colleague, intellect, closet comedian, and the list goes on and on and on.

Constantly running from labeling myself as a rape victim used immense amounts of energy. By owning the label, I was able to redirect my energy into different areas of my life. My relationships took on new depth and meaning because I was able to allocate more of myself to them. As I began to use the tools and grace offered by my mind, spirit, and body, the color of my flower started to change, just as the wise spiritual healer had suggested. As I owned every piece of me with love, the people drawn into my life were also holding me in the highest regard: partners, friends, and family.

My ability to live authentically and in my truth is still the greatest gift I've ever received. Acknowledging that the sexual assault was affecting my ability to build meaningful relationships was the best first step I have ever taken. It led me to embrace change from within and build a beautiful new relationship with my mind, spirit, and body. As the three started to communicate with each other, magic happened. It made me beautifully whole and allowed me to have a life with truly meaningful relationships.

This information is not provided to implicate life is always perfect. There is beauty in the imperfection, and learning to use these tools on a daily basis has supported myself and others in experiencing tremendous growth and transformation. Problems do and will arise. And that is okay.

Chapter 9
If the Magic Seems to Fade

Pure magic is the only way I know how to describe life after learning to connect to myself wholly. With that being said, it does not mean old belief systems and self-doubt do not try to creep back into my life. The only difference is now I'm better prepared to handle it when it does.

There are days I still feel defeated, and the old ways of thinking creep into my mind. By listening to my mind, spirit, and body, I have the tools to support the disruption of those creeping thoughts. And on days when I feel I do not have the ability to disrupt them, I choose to fully love the parts of me not feeling very lovely. Love can come in many shapes and forms. If I'm really down and can't get out of the negative headspace, a warm bath surrounded by candles often does the trick to love my broken soul. When I do the traditional fall to the kitchen floor sobbing, sometimes a good book with a little ice cream is just what the body has ordered. Netflix and chill is also a great option: a mindless show and a few giggles are great for the soul.

When I just need to talk, I have built the most beautiful support system. On any given day, I know there are over a dozen people I can call and say, "Please listen. " This shift represents a huge change from how I used to live my life. I'm no longer isolated and alone. I have the meaningful relationships necessary to make it through the tough days. Each relationship is based on the reciprocity of love and support.

On the ten-year anniversary of being sexually assaulted, I made the decision to begin rewriting my life story. I was tired of the annual sleepless, anxious nights and anticipating being woken up in the middle of the night with the fear of being raped. I was tired of not being able to explain why I became more quirky and aloof to colleagues and friends year after year. I was desperate to try something new.

The first year I tried to rewrite my story, I trained for a 5K that just so happened to be on the exact ten-year anniversary of the rape. Now to some a 5K is simple, something you do for fun and super easy. For me, the 5K was one of the most difficult things I have accomplished in my life. It was not just a run. It was an attempt to heal on a deeper level. I proudly posted my progress on social media daily.

Everyone thought they were cheering me on to run a simple race. They had no clue they were cheering me on as I tried to rewrite the story of my life. Although I was not fast and many days I felt defeated, running became my obsession.

As my mind tried to tell me how stupid I was for doing this activity, my body craved the release from anxiety I experienced each time that I hit the pavement. My anxiety lessened, and sleep became easier. The better sleep I got helped to clear my clouded mind. There were days I would finish a run and go home to sob. My body was communicating, but I was not sure what it was saying. I would visual journal and then go along with life.

My sister, Chelsey, made the four-and-a-half-hour drive over to run this silly race with me. She knew how hard I worked to try to change my story. We trotted side by side in the beautiful park in western Washington. She is actually a runner, so the poor girl had to slow down to my pace. Nonetheless, we made it to the finish line. The joy in my heart was unexplainable. *I did it!* I freaking did something healthy and positive on the anniversary of the rape. I did not stay in bed and hide from the world. I did not cry and anxiously hide in fear. I freaking ran a 5K!

After the ten-year anniversary, I knew I needed to do the same for the following years. Being someone who has always had stomach issues, I chose to do a thirty-day diet where I eliminated foods that cause inflammation. My mother and a few of my girlfriends decided to join in. I was relentlessly dedicated to this diet. There was no way I would cheat or fail. Because for me this was not about just a diet, this was about learning to listen to my body in a different way.

Once again, this new adventure was posted to social media. I even made a closed group on a social media platform for us to support each other. Very few knew why this diet meant so much to me. Frankly it didn't matter if they did. I knew this was another way for me to make a healthy choice on the anniversary of the rape, and I would let nothing come in the way of it.

By the end of the thirty days, I felt healthier, happier, and like I had conquered another milestone. The rape was no longer the only event that had occurred in the month of May. I now had memories of being a 5K runner and having the drive to commit to a thirty-day restrictive diet that supported me to learn about my food intolerances. You better believe I celebrated with a whole gluten-free cheese pizza on day thirty-one! Maybe the decision was counterproductive to the purpose of the diet, but for me this process was more than a diet. It was about rewriting my story and making another healthy, positive choice. As great as the diet was, the most memorable part was the pizza at the end of the story.

The following year was my favorite choice of all. During the anniversary week of the rape, I booked a trip to one of my favorite places in the world, Newport, Rhode Island. It was there I had originally met with so many of the healers and change makers who supported me on this path. This particular year was all about getting in connection with my core. What was next for Melissa and how was she going to get there? I took the time to meet with wise mentors, have a Rosen Method Session, and a Rolfing session, met with a psychic medium, and laughed and cried with my dear friends Ashley and Erica around the kitchen table.

For information on the Rosen Method and Rolfing please see the websites below.

- Rosen Method: http://rosenmethod.com
- Rolfing: https://rolf.org

In every conversation and healing session, all roads pointed me to write and tell my story in order to help others in their healing. It was time to stop living two lives: the one I thought I needed to portray and the one hid behind closed doors. It was time to give myself the grace to come out of hiding and fully live.

Writing has been my jam ever since I can remember. I was writing books and poetry as an elementary student. As a young girl, I mostly I wrote about the magical man on the moon and the girl on the ground with my grandfather. Together we processed my parent's divorce and I learned tools to make sense of my inner world through writing. Writing is the way my sweet spirit conveys its deepest truth and has freedom to breathe.

The recovery from and the ability to build meaningful relationships after sexual assault represents an ongoing process. Sexual assault is an extremely personal experience. There are no two stories that are the same and no two people who are going to heal in the exact same way. The only constant I would argue is we each have a mind, spirit, and body, and each of those pieces are affected by sexual assault.

Learning to listen to your mind, spirit, and body and the way they interact together will help you in supporting your healing. Knowing when you need to take a bath in solitude or to call your best friend and have a cry session are crucial elements in your ability to progress or move forward. On the days where you feel down and defeated, honor those feelings with love. If you try to rewrite your story and feel as if it can't be rewritten, honor those feelings with love. The more love you meet yourself with, the more love will start coming back to you.

It took me ten freaking years before I was ready to rewrite my story. That ten-year period represented years of tears, anxiety, and hopelessness. Don't wait ten years to get your life back.

Let's lovingly take back your power now! If you have waited ten plus years, there is no better time than now to lovingly take back your power. This life is yours and sexual assault may be a part of your story, but it most definitely is not your entire story.

- *You have a beautiful body ready to be loved and respected, not only by yourself but also by others.*
- *You have a brilliant mind capable of ditching those beliefs not serving you.*
- *You have a fierce inner voice (spirit) ready to speak up and share its deepest fears and desires.*
- *You have amazingly kind people in this world ready and waiting to love you. You are so loved!*

On the days where you fall to the kitchen floor crying and do not know where to turn, turn to me. Turn to this book. Turn to love. Love is the only thing real in this crazy universe. It is the only thing that is going to help you move from feelings of isolation and loneliness and into a life of abundant meaningful relationships. Being sexually assaulted can make it seem as if everything good in the world has been stolen from you.

Heck, to me, being sexually assaulted felt truly as a theft. It was a theft of my right to give my body to whomever I pleased. It was a theft of my ability to trust. It was a theft of my ability to love others and myself. I was tired of feeling stolen from and wanted to get those parts back. All roads led me to love. The ability to lovingly be able to give my body to others, to trust people and myself, and to give/receive love was built on my new relationships with self-love.

Chapter 10
Dance with Me

Let's venture back to the Tanzanian spiritual healer's beautiful garden. After the healer's analogy of honeybees and flowers, he asked me to join my *dadas*, Carly and Doc Daver, in the small shed with beautiful stained glass windows.

Once in the shed, we were asked to draw whatever came to mind with colored pencils. Feeling a bit silly, I drew a picture of a tree with stick figure dancers below. The dancers were in the grass looking toward a small pond. In the sky was a cloud with my name written in it. My drawing skills are equally as fantastic as my dancing skills. Think two-year-old in a tutu again.

Once the picture was completed, I was asked to share its meaning. "There is a tree, dancers, a cloud, and a pond," I proudly stated.

Perplexed by the vague description, the spiritual healer asked me to try again. "What more could there be to this picture?" *Ugh.*

I tried again. "There is a tall tree with branches high above the multicolored dancers. The small cloud in the sky had my name Melissa written in it. The small blue pond drifted off the page."

The spiritual healer was not impressed. He decided to help me out and offer his wisdom again, claiming, "Melissa, the tree represents you and your large grounded presence. The dancers represent how people are drawn to your presence. Can you tell me why the dancers are not holding hands? What would life look like if you used your ability to bring people together with the purpose of building connection?"

My mind was blown. I still did not fully understand where he was going with this analogy. I sat in awe, though. Uncertain of the answer, my *dadas* and I jumped into the white safari truck and giggled our way home.

Years went by, and the healer's words were a distant memory. My final quarter of graduate school, the *aha* moment happened. As we sat in our sacred circle dialoguing about the work of leadership scholars who had come before us, the wise healer's words came flooding back and hit me smack in the face.

When light is shined on our darkest parts, it is often a rude awakening as the light peeks in. Until this moment, I lived on a soapbox, touting myself as an anomaly—truly believing no one, especially women who had experienced the trauma I have and come out on top. This tool served a great purpose in my life for some time.

Hiding my pain from others felt somewhat like a superpower. I was living an undercover life. The only time I gave others glimpses of my world was for them to share in my accomplishments and travels. If I felt remotely off or triggered because of the sexual assault, I would go into hiding, only returning if I had the ability to hide my pain.

Separating myself and hiding my pain was not supporting me to build meaningful relationships. In fact, my have-it-all-together attitude made me less likely to make friends. I was a fake person living in a real world.

There were so many acquaintances around me, just like the dancers beneath the tree. I never wanted to connect with them because I was worried I would lose my superpower hiding skills. One of the dancers may "out me" and I did not know how to handle that.

Sitting in class that day, I realized it was time to help people dance together through this thing we call life. It was time to learn how to help others connect, just as the spiritual healer in Tanzania had asked me to do for the dancers in the picture.

The introspective questions were terrifying: "What will I look like off my soapbox? Will I blend into the crowd? Are people going to judge me because I have been sexually assaulted?"

Slowly, I gave vulnerability a try, in safe spaces and small doses. I found myself being surrounded by love as I shared my truth authentically. Instead of disappearing into the crowd, I began to shine. My gifts lit up as I allowed myself to jump off my soapbox and fit into the whole collective of other sexual assault victims. The pressure of feeling like I had to fight this battle lessened as the weight was shared and carried by others.

By stepping back and learning how to fit in the whole, I was able to let others step up on the soapbox and shine. We each have so many beautiful gifts to share with those whom we are in relationships with. There is no greater gift than to support others on their path to living their authentic life with truth and in relationship with others.

My inability to see myself for the beautiful woman I was hindered my ability to build meaningful relationships. The love I found for myself in mind, spirit, and body opened my eyes to how they work in my world individually. As wonderful as they are separately, though, the real magic happens when they work relationally to one another.

The relationship to my mind and the negative self-talk was attracting those who also thought poorly of me. The minute I started recognizing my thoughts had power over my ability to build relationships, a weight was lifted from my shoulders. As I began to hold the negative thoughts and spaces in my mind with love, I began to attract others into my life who held my thoughts with love.

The relationship with my sweet spirit had been lost after sexual assault. This transpired not only from the assault, but also from having a religious figure listen to my story in disbelief, which left a very bitter taste for me to sample anything religious or spiritually related. Learning religion and spirituality are not a both/and relationship gave me the freedom to connect to my spirit in a way that made sense to me. I now can dance and pray to the goddess within just as my little girl self would do. By learning to communicate with my spirit, I have the ability to listen to my intuition and live with more grace for others.

The relationship with my body was the most damaged of all. I used my relationship with my mind to constantly beat it up, so much so I felt like it was a stranger just along for the ride of my life. As I began to listen to its language and communicate with it on a deeper level, I learned it is a majestic being. Dancing naked in front of the mirror, there was nothing but glory. Learning to speak with my body has supported my healing growth by leaps and bounds. The visual journaling as a tool to speak to my body has turned into a sacred dialogue.

Without the ability to connect with my mind, spirit, and body, I would not have the ability to connect with others. Holding each part of myself with the utmost love and respect sets the stage for how others can treat me. No longer do I find myself attracting negativity as I did before. If I do see negativity coming my way, I have the tools to lessen and deter its effects.

So what about the dancers? You, my loves, are the dancers. Now is the time, more than ever, to start the dialogue about life after sexual assault. It is time we start holding the space for us to dance in our underwear, laugh as we blow snot bubbles, and learn what is no longer serving us. It is my personal mission to support other sexual assault victims in feeling that you are seen, heard, and loved. I want to help you find your inner goddess and let your true authentic self shine.

I invite you to take my hand and start this dance with me.

Beautiful reader, please know: I see you. I hear you. I love you. I am you.

Love,
Melissa Ann

About the Author

 **Melissa Ann McDaniel** is a sexual assault survivor turned personal empowerment coach. Drawing from her own transformational experience and educational background, she supports women to build the meaningful relationships they crave after sexual assault. Melissa holds a master of arts degree in holistic leadership and has additional training in the creative and expressive arts. She is currently a doctoral student in leadership studies. Melissa was featured in *TOI Magazine's* April 2019 issue for Sexual Assault Awareness Month. She currently resides in Spokane, Washington.